# ENLIGHTENED
# Retirement

A Guide for Boomers Who Want to Live Large
and Change the World in Their Retirement Years

## Susan Steiner

### 2013

For Abe and all our grandchildren

The author gratefully acknowledges the following people for their inspiration, support, expertise, friendship and general hand-holding. Natalie Goldberg, who taught me to write; Scott Edelstein, editor extraordinaire; my sister Bonnie, who supports every dream I have; the friends who stand by me no matter what – Valerie, Sheryl, Kathy, and Lori; Kristi, the daughter of my heart; and most of all AJ, for more than words can say. Thanks to all.

# ENLIGHTENED
# Retirement

A Guide for Boomers Who Want to Live Large
and Change the World in Their Retirement Years

---

Your Grand Future ..................................................................... 1

I.   **Your foundation** ................................................................ 7
     You are unique ................................................................. 7
     You have gifts and talents ................................................. 10
     You persevere ................................................................ 13
     You have much to share ..................................................... 16
     The power of small steps ................................................... 19
     Going with the flow ......................................................... 22

II.  **Your Outer World** ........................................................... 27
     Home ........................................................................ 28
     Time and play ............................................................... 31
     Health ...................................................................... 34
     Money ....................................................................... 37
     Society ..................................................................... 40

III. **Your Inner World** ........................................................... 43
     We are transformers ......................................................... 43
     Gathering lessons ........................................................... 46
     Dream makers ................................................................ 49
     Relationships ............................................................... 52
     Universal connections ....................................................... 55
     What does the world need from you? .......................................... 58

IV.  **Synthesizing and Manifesting** ................................... **61**
    Creating ........................................................ 61
    Meditating .................................................... 64
    Manifesting peace ........................................ 67

V.  **Your Unique Legacy** ....................................... **71**
    Question everything – again ..................... 71
    Fearless thinking ......................................... 75
    Tell your story ............................................. 78

VI.  **Do What You Can From Where You Are** .................. **81**
    Acts of kindness ......................................... 81
    Gratitude ...................................................... 84

**Seeker, Pathfinder, Guardian** ..................................... **87**

**Appendix: Recommended "How to" Retirement Resources** ........ **89**

# Your Grand Future

---

We're the Baby Boomers – 78 million strong in the United States alone. We came in on a wave of post-WWII exhaustion, rebuilding, and prosperity. We confounded our parents, embraced rock and roll, made jeans a national uniform, protested the VietNam war, and spoke with fire, passion, love, vision, and dreams. We had a look, a style, a music, and a voice.

Do you hear that voice now? Sure the music is still there. Jagger still swaggers, the Eagles soar again, and Springsteen still gets us out of our seats. The clothes are still there, too. Everyone wears jeans, baseball caps are ubiquitous, business attire for men hasn't included hats since JFK's bare-headed inauguration, and our grandkids wear hip-hugging bellbottoms.

We also had a vision for the world that was in some ways as powerful and radical as the vision America's Founding Fathers held when they created the U.S. Constitution. Maybe each of us only held a piece of the vision, but we came together with a passion for changing what didn't seem right and for making a different, better world.

As we approach retirement with greater health, resources, power, and sheer numbers than any previous generation, are we really satisfied to remain silent? Do we have any sense of a life unfinished?

Most of us can look forward to 20-30 retirement years of health, security, and leisure. What if that is just the *beginning*? What if during the last two decades you have built a foundation from which you can launch your greatest legacy? What if you are not done, but are only just starting to fulfill your promise?

What if you have been quietly gathering maturity and strength to raise your voice once more for what really matters, for something bigger than yourself, for this battered and glorious world we inhabit?

What if you are now, in your maturity, coming into your full power as a visionary and a world-changer? What if you have been in a state of quiet spiritual evolution – like a caterpillar in a cocoon? What if your retirement is when you re-emerge as the spiritual warrior you felt yourself to be in your youth?

Somewhere inside each of us, isn't the dream still alive? Can't you still see the vision? Isn't it possible that we came in together as a big, brash, raucous generation because we were given something special to do – something the world still needs?

Welcome to *Enlightened Retirement*. This book will help you discover not only how to have a fun and happy retirement, but how to create meaning for yourself and for those coming behind you. It will help you fulfill – or reclaim – your legacy by helping at least one person, or one family, or one group to reach for their dream.

If we are going to help our children find their dreams, we need to live our own. We need to include *our* heart's dream in our ideal retirement – give it size, shape, and structure, and make it real. Doing this can model for our children what living a dream looks like.

Dreams are magnetic and magic; they lift us up, connect us spiritually, and have the power to change the world. Our children need to know our dreams, need to hear our hearts speaking, need to believe in the power of one person to make a difference for many.

We still have the clothes, we still have the music, we still have the memories. And now, in retirement, we have the leisure, the resources, and the wisdom to stand at the gates of the land where our dreams live, hold them open, and show our children the path.

This is not a nuts-and-bolts book that will tell you where to invest your money, how to locate a great doctor, or what cities are ideal places to retire. Other books on retirement already cover those topics quite well. See the Appendix for a list of some of the best of these..

Rather, *Enlightened Retirement* is a companion book to each of those nuts-and-bolts guides. It's a guide to your own heart, hopes, and dreams as you begin to look toward retirement. It's a meditation on who you are and who you want to be in your retirement years. And it's a process of inquiry that will help you focus on what is most important as you move from a life centered on work and family into the retirement of your dreams.

You will find journal pages throughout this book. You can use them to make your own notes, drawings, and lists as you discover your dreams and visions for living an enlightened retirement. Or, if you prefer, buy a separate journal to carry with you as you read this book. Each section of *Enlightened Retirement* offers you an opportunity to record your thoughts if you wish, or to simply meditate and reflect on the topic at hand. Whatever your choice, let your imagination and dreams take you on a journey of exploring your ideal, enlightened retirement.

Tomorrow awaits. Join me in a class reunion where we remember how we were young together, embrace all that we've accomplished so far, and use our maturity and wisdom to build a foundation for the kind of future we believe is possible.

Throughout this book, any reference to "children" includes all those people who come behind us: sons, daughters, nieces, nephews, grandchildren, students, etc.

# I.

# Your Foundation

---

## YOU ARE UNIQUE

There is no one else exactly like you, anywhere on Earth in this time or any other.

In the pages to come, you'll look at the ways in which you are unique, special, and needed in the world.

As you approach your full maturity, you have accumulated a stunning list of accomplishments, among them some or all of the following:

- surviving your teenage years and moving out of your parents' house

- getting educated, or professionally trained

- starting a job, learning to support yourself, and building a career

- finding a spouse or partner

- starting a family

- making a home

- raising your child(ren)

- getting your child(ren) educated or professionally trained

- tending to your aging parents

- achieving some degree of professional stature

- setting aside money for your future

- setting and reaching a variety of goals

As you read this list, take time to savor and acknowledge the magnitude of what you have done. Each of these achievements took energy, determination, planning, perseverance, resilience, often some luck, and perhaps help from friends and/or family. Each likely created some laughter and tears, heartbreak and exhilaration, stops and starts. Each not only made you stronger and braver, but touched others' lives as well.

These are not accomplishments to be taken for granted, but ones to appreciate and acknowledge. Read the above list aloud so you can hear your own voice speaking your truth into the world.

Then use the following page, or your own journal, to add to this list as you remember the path you have traveled to get to where you are today.

As you think about creating a meaningful retirement, refer to this list as a reminder that you are already unique and capable. The same life skills that have helped you accomplish so much are waiting to help you accomplish the retirement life of your dreams.

If you're like many other members of our generation, you want to leave your mark; you want to inspire your children and grandchildren; you want to go out with bang, not a whimper. For that, you need the energy of your dreams. Where are they? What is their language? How can you recapture or create them? How can you use them to make a plan for retirement that will fill you to overflowing?

All that you have accomplished so far in your life has created a toolbox full of skills, knowledge, and connections that you are uniquely equipped to use. The world needs you and this toolbox, and the piece of the vision you hold for leaving the world better for your children and grandchildren.

## *What I have accomplished in my life*

## YOU HAVE GIFTS AND TALENTS

Imagine your life as a movie. Your stumbles and heartbreaks are not failures, but lessons learned along the way – things that happened to make you stronger and better prepared for what came next. Your successes and triumphs show where you stood tall, persevered, and honored the intention of your spirit.

By the time we reach our 50s, we've been learning, experimenting, and mastering all kinds of skills for decades. A lot of the stuff we did as kids was actually preparing us for life. Remember the kid in fifth grade who could play music with his armpit? He might have gone on to become a successful musician – or a successful comedian. The kid who spent every study hall drawing sports cars in his notebook may have gone on to design cars at Ford. The girl who rescued every stray kitten and lost pup may today be a prominent veterinarian. What we loved to do when we were young is often what we become good at when we're older. And what we loved then is usually a message about what we still love today, and what calls us to dream.

Everyone can do some things very well. Ironically, it is often those things we love most and do best that we most take for granted and discount as "no big deal." We often envy what others seem good at, without taking the time to look at our own skills.

Sometimes what we're good at has evolved so gradually over time that we haven't noticed that we were practicing and accumulating experience. We're like the figure skater who finally learns to carve a perfect figure 8 with grace and ease, after missing it a thousand times.

If part of our quest is to show our children and grandchildren how to make their own dreams come alive, it is useful to know what we do best and can teach most effectively. Clues to our skills lie everywhere, if only we will take the time to pause, consider, and acknowledge what we have learned and can do well.

Think about the ways in which family and friends rely upon you. Pretend that those qualities are a job description. Are you a chef, an organizational expert, a budget analyst, a landscape designer, an interior decorator, an animal trainer, a safety consultant, a master scheduler, a child psychologist, a conflict negotiator?

Think about who you are at work, and what people there rely on you for. Beyond the basic work requirements, you are likely appreciated for other qualities. Can you think of times when people at work have thanked you for something special, or enlisted your help? What you do is about the job; but how you do it is about your unique gifts and talents.

Which of your gifts and talents would you most enjoy rediscovering, refining, and sharing with others? Where does the world need the skills and experience you have spent a lifetime accumulating and practicing? How can the sum of all you have learned and mastered become the light you shine into the world as a retiree?

On the following page, or in your journal, write a list of your special skills, gifts, and talents. This is your personal job description of all those qualities people rely on and value about you.

We are conditioned by family, society, and each other to downplay our abilities, as if acknowledging them would be arrogant. But if you think of your skills and experience as resources you have been accumulating for a time when they will be needed, you can see them more fully and clearly – and you can more readily offer them to the world. For the world *does* need your know-how, now more than ever.

If you were suddenly called upon to use your skills to help in an emergency, you would know what to do without hesitation. Our dream to leave this world better for our children is no less compelling, and calls us to use the full power of our skills and experience to create a retirement that summons and reflects the best we have to give.

## *What people count on me for*

## YOU PERSEVERE

Many of us remember watching those commercials with John Cameron Swayze and the indestructible watch that took a lickin' and kept on tickin'. Think about yourself as that watch – buffeted and banged around by life, but enduring and persevering. You have learned to rely on yourself, to trust that you will keep going, and to see that the down times are more than balanced by the good and happy times. Your resilience is essential in creating a solid foundation for a family, a career, a life, a dream, a world.

Think of a time very early in your life when you triumphed through something difficult or challenging. For most of us, one of those first times might be learning to ride a two-wheel bicycle. Can you remember how wobbly it felt, how shaky the handlebars were, how your feet kept slipping off the pedals, how someone jogged alongside, holding the seat, so you didn't lose your balance? And do you remember the exhilaration and thrill when you realized no one was holding you steady anymore and you were riding on your own?

What other times can you recall when you mastered something that seemed impossible at first, because you kept going? Was it learning a musical instrument, doing long division, tying a perfect necktie, hitting a straight shot off the tee, baking a fluffy soufflé, or knitting your first sweater? Think about the many things you can now do because you persevered and were resilient in the face of difficulty.

In addition to mastering challenges in the physical world, we each call upon the power of resiliency in our emotional lives. From small disappointments to large heartbreaks, you have learned to persevere, to keep going, to pick yourself up and start again. Can you recall something you really wanted, had your heart set on, that you didn't get, but then you reached inside yourself for strength and courage, and kept right on going? Can you reflect on and appreciate those times when you pulled yourself through something hurtful or difficult and gained the satisfaction of knowing that you were strong and resilient?

Our parents gave us living examples for coping with life, and we have expanded on their examples as we teach our children. Being resilient and coping with life are skills that we use in big and small ways. And often we don't acknowledge them as part of our inner strength.

- How do you behave around an unruly child? Do you remain calm and try to help the child settle down?

- How do you react when someone cuts you off in traffic? Are you able to maintain your focus on safe driving?

- How do you react when someone at work makes a mistake that affects your own performance, or creates more work for you? Do you calmly address the issue as a human phenomenon that affects us all?

- How do you act when someone in your family is upset? Do you offer understanding and a neutral space for talking about the issue?

- What coping skills do people look to you for? How do others rely on you in dealing with stress or problems?

- What coping skills would you most like your children to have as adults? How can you help them develop and practice those skills?

As you ponder these questions, make notes on the following page, or in your journal, about the many ways you have persevered in your life.

Consider what you have learned about pushing through, holding steadfast, and persevering. How can you engage these qualities in pursuit of your dream retirement? Where do you see the need for the coping skills – the resilience – you have mastered? Who around you can you share your life skills with? How can your retirement be a testament to the power of perseverance in keeping your dreams alive – your dreams for yourself, your children, and the world?

## *Ways I have persevered*

## YOU HAVE MUCH TO SHARE

In the previous section you looked at your personal attributes that are the tools you can use to change the world. You can leverage these to build a retirement that is happy and fulfilling.

For example, what you know and can do are timeless assets that increase your happiness when you share them with others. Use the following questions, expanding on them if you like, to make a list of the many ways you can share of yourself. Write your list on the following page or in your personal journal.

- If public speaking, management, or fund-raising was a part of your work life, can you use those abilities on behalf of your favorite charity, to start a neighborhood community center, to improve the local animal shelter, to get a new playground for the local day care center, or to start a food donation program with local restaurants? Can you think of other ways to transfer your workplace skills into community activities?

- If gardening has been your passion, can you work with your local government to find some public land for a community garden? Can you develop a simple manual for beginning gardeners on using regional plants and grasses? Can you volunteer to teach simple gardening techniques in a local school or community center? Where near you does the world need the beauty of growing flowers, or the bounty of easy-to-grow vegetables?

- Are you good at organizing an office? If so, can you volunteer for a local charity?

- Can you sew, build birdhouses, bake, or repair household appliances? Where are there children in your community who would like to learn what you know? Where are there elderly people who would be happy for those services and your company?

- What are the issues that concern you, that you feel passionate about? Can you make a small monthly donation to that cause? Can you vote for legislators who support it? Can you find a local action group that is working on it? Can you write editorials or letters about it for your local newspaper or community tv station?

- Can you share of yourself in some entirely new and valuable way?

What we have to share can be large or small, long-lasting or brief, local or global. Sharing something of yourself, your knowledge, and your talent keeps you connected with your purpose and with the dream we all share to make things better.

How can you make sharing a part of your retirement plan? Who needs your knowledge and wisdom? What cause needs your time or resources? How can you make your retirement about sharing the blessings and joys of your life?

## *What I can share: wisdom, knowledge and skills*

## THE POWER OF SMALL STEPS

The power of small steps to make big changes is easy to overlook. Yet a small, gentle trickle of water dropping continually in the same spot can wear a hole right through rock.

When we think about the power we have to make change, we often focus on the big splashy actions that have a lot of noise and visibility. Not all of us can change the world in a big, splashy way. But each of us has the ability, and the power, to be the steady trickle of water wearing through the rock, to take small and gentle actions that will change the people and the world around us.

- Think of a small gesture you have done that made a difference in someone's day. Did you take a friend to lunch on the spur of the moment? Did you send someone a "thinking of you" card just to stay in touch? Did you bake a cake for your family when there was no special occasion? Did you mow the lawn for the neighbors when they were out of town? Did you see someone struggling to load groceries into the car and offer to help? Each day offers us opportunities to acknowledge that we're all connected in this world.

- There are always small things you can do in your family, or in your circle of friends, to say "I love you." You can cook someone's favorite meal; replace a worn blanket with a new soft one; plant flowers outside the window where everyone sits to eat; tuck a special note inside a child's lunch box; offer to help a friend move without being asked; make soup for someone with a cold; offer to accompany a friend to a doctor's appointment; or surprise someone with a bouquet of fresh flowers. Making these small actions regular parts of your life will help you develop a practice of using small steps to make a big impact.

- Can you think of times when someone's small action or gesture made a difference in your own life? Who in your family has done something special for you? Do you have a friend you can always count on, no matter what?

- Have you been especially moved by something a stranger did or said? How did you feel when that happened? Is that a feeling you would like to invoke in someone else?

When we are the recipient of someone's small gesture, it often feels quite big to us. That is the power of small steps – someone's word or deed says to us, "I care; I'm here; you're not alone."

Think of ways you can routinely make those small connections with someone, and make notes on the following page or in your journal.

## *Small actions I can take for other people and the world*

_____

## GOING WITH THE FLOW

Any one of us who has tried to teach an elderly parent how to use a cell phone or a computer knows how much the world has changed in our lifetime, and how much we take for granted. We Boomers have demonstrated an ability to embrace change, make it our own, and keep going. Collectively and individually we have adapted in mid-stride, often on the run, and lived out one of our own early adages: go with the flow. That ability to adapt to change will allow us to move elegantly into retirement and make it meaningful and rewarding.

Think about some of the ways you have faced and adapted to change, and how you can use those adaptations and skills in retirement. As you ponder these questions, make notes on the following page or in your journal.

- Think back to your childhood. What was the first big change you remember in your family relationships? Did a new brother or sister arrive and disrupt your world? How did you feel about this newcomer, and did your parents help you adjust? Do you recall a particular moment when you accepted your new sibling into your life?

- Can you remember the first person whose death affected you? How did you cope with this loss? Were there understanding people around to help you cope, or did you face your grieving alone?

- Do you remember your first best friend? Is that person still your best friend? If not, do you recall how you dealt with the change in your friendship? What have you learned about selecting and sustaining connections as you observe the way important friendships change over time?

- Do you have good friends who live in other parts of the country (or the world)? How do you maintain your connection with them? How have you adapted to stay close over the distance? What steps can you take to assure that your primary friendships can be maintained in retirement?

- Are you helping your children understand the constancy of change and how to adapt to it? Have you helped them weather changes in friendships, the loss of a pet, or the death of a family member? Are you using your own experience in managing change to help them adapt? Their lives will likely experience even more profound changes than yours; how are you helping them learn to accept the inevitable changes in their lives?

- Do you have a vision of yourself handling life's changes with inner calm? What might you do to achieve that state of peace? Does this involve a spiritual practice, exercise, meditation, nature, or loving relationships? Can you think of specific instances where you met challenges or changes with equanimity and calm? Are you helping your children learn ways of achieving their own serenity?

- We all have to face change, but we don't have to face it alone. Think about the people who play important roles in your life. Who are good advisors and confidants for you as you prepare for retirement? Who can go to for help when you really need it? Who are you are willing to drop everything for if they call on you?

- On the following page, or in your journal, write out these people's full contact information and make notes about their relationship to you and why they are special to you. Placing such a list with your important papers will help your family contact these people on your behalf if and when necessary.

The world we have grown up and matured in has called us to be adaptable and flexible. We have learned to surf the waves of change and to accept that change is a constant. Unlike previous generations of retirees, we have the choice and the freedom to remain fluid and engaged. From your vantage point as an accomplished and active elder, you can model how to go with the flow, and in the process have fun, stay engaged, and make retirement the best time of your life.

## *How I go with the flow – and who I want with me*

# II.

# Your Outer World

---

In the previous pages you spent time considering all that you have learned and experienced. You may now be reconnecting with some of your old energy, dreams, and power. You are beginning to sense that there is more you want to do, to be, to learn, and to share – that your life's work is not finished. While these thoughts are percolating, let's turn for a short time to what your outer life will look like in retirement. This includes home, time, play, health, money, and society.

The changes that retirement may bring to your physical world can have a surprisingly large emotional impact. You may be considering a smaller home, a more relaxed wardrobe, or a smaller car. Though we know in our heads that happiness comes more from who we are than what we have, we may feel strong attachments to the material parts of our life. Be gentle with yourself as you consider your reasons and feelings for making changes.

## HOME

As you face retirement, you have the resources, mobility, and inclination to think about where and how you want to live. The internet, e-mail, and frequent flyer miles can keep you connected to your family and your friends in ways unimagined by your parents. You can live just about anywhere, and stay connected to just about anywhere else. Still, your decision may be driven in part by a wish to live close (or closer) to children or aging parents.

Take some time to envision your ideal retirement home. This is primarily a dreaming process, so for the moment put aside restrictions about affordability, interest rates, mortgage commitments, etc. Allow your dream retirement home to reveal itself to you; later on you can shape it with practical considerations. On the following page, or in your journal, write down or draw your ideas, additional thoughts, and new questions that may emerge.

- Are you content in the community where you now live, or do you envision living somewhere else? Do you want a change in the neighborhood? The climate? The local economy? What would these changes be?

- Is the upkeep on your current home something you're willing to handle for the next 20+ years? If not, do you want to stay put and make renovations that will lessen maintenance, or move to something less demanding?

- Are you OK with the environmental impact of the home you have now? Is there a way to have the home of your dreams and also have a lower impact on the environment?

- What kinds of activities would you love to have within easy walking or driving distance? Are these activities you can do alone, or would you do them with other people? Where might you live so that these activities and people are easily accessible?

- How near do you want to live to goods and services you prefer – medical and personal care, big malls or neighborhood shops, grocery stores or markets, nightlife, museums and galleries, organized sports?

- Have you dreamed of traveling in a home on wheels or in the water? If so, envision this home in detail.

It is true that "home is where the heart is." What is your heart telling you about where and how you want to live in retirement?

# *My dream retirement home*

## TIME AND PLAY

Once you fully retire, you will have days, weeks, and months of free time to spend. Those of us who don't prepare for it can find this deep pool of time daunting. Sometimes they are so unprepared that they end up sitting by the side rather than diving in.

You can use your retirement time more productively and happily by reflecting on and recalling what kind of play most appeals to you. I encourage you to mentally review your life, year by year, and recall what kind of play most satisfied you at each stage. Then consider how you can play in a similar way in retirement. Here are some examples:

- The little boy who galloped a broom around the yard yelling "giddyup" may, in retirement, volunteer in an equine rescue center or join a riding club.

- The little girl who lined up all her dolls in a make-believe school and taught them the alphabet may volunteer as an adopt-a-grandma at a local elementary school.

- The man who played weekend golf for 20 years may want to work part-time at the local course.

- The mom who loved baking cookies for her kids may want to teach gourmet cookie design at a community center.

Here are some fun – and enlightening – questions to ask yourself about play. As you consider them, make notes on the following page or in your journal.

- Remember a time from your childhood when you were completely absorbed in play. What were you doing? Were you indoors or outside? Were you alone, with a good friend, or with a group of children?

- Did you especially enjoy playing at something that required some skill, such as skating, swimming, painting, or tennis?

- Find the adult version of what the kid in you loved to do. If you loved art projects when you were young, find a local art supply store and pick out some things that look fun to try. If your favorite winter activity as a child was sledding, buy or borrow a sled and start hurtling down snow-covered hills again. Make a few play dates with yourself to remember (or discover) what feels fun, interesting, joyful. Dedicate three to four hours exploring something you'd like to play at.

- How structured do you like your play? Do you prefer putting fun things on your calendar?

- Do you want to do them on a regular, scheduled basis so you can look forward to them and plan around them? Or do you prefer an unscheduled lifestyle where each day offers you fresh opportunities and choices? Or will you thrive on some combination?

Play slows time down, puts you squarely in the present moment, and connects you with the energy and imagination that comes so naturally to children. Using your well-earned retirement time to engage in play is far from frivolous; it is an important part of your retirement happiness.

## *Kinds of play I have enjoyed – and new things I want to try*

## HEALTH

It's never too late to give yourself a better retirement by taking good care of yourself.

Think of yourself as a well-designed crystal pitcher that wants to pour out resources to self, family, friends, and community. With good self-care, you can keep that pitcher full and always ready to give.

But a pitcher that is not adequately cared for will crack and leak – and, as a result, will not have enough to share.

Your self-care includes tending not only to your body, but also to your mind and spirit. You may eat well, but if you're constantly stressed, you may end up with a stomach ache. And if you have not established a way to connect with your spiritual side, you may always feel a little empty, no matter how much you eat.

Accept your health for what it is now, then begin to make small changes. The body, spirit, and mind strive for balance, and whatever investment of time and energy you make in health now will help prepare you for an active, enjoyable retirement.

Better health is available to all of us, at all times, at whatever level we can manage. We took health for granted when we were young; we can take it as our responsibility now. Think about what your personal best health can be in body, mind, and heart. Write about or draw it on the following page, or in your journal.

Then consider how you can begin moving toward it by taking those small, consistent steps that you know how to take. How might your retirement years be enhanced if you begin now (or continue) to make health a priority? Write down your thoughts on both of these subjects.

Consider some of these questions as well:

- Was there a time in your life when you were in perfect health? When was that? What were you doing then to maintain your health? What were you eating? Were you exercising regularly? How did it feel to be really healthy?

- What is your family history of health and illness? Of your sib-lings, parents, and grandparents, which ones enjoyed the best health, and what habits did they practice to support that health? Are there any serious or chronic illnesses in your family?

- Do you know the internal rhythms and cycles of your body? What foods does your body tell you to avoid, or to eat more of? What messages does it give you about the amount of sleep you need, the degree of stress you can handle, and the amount of exertion that may lead to soreness or injury? What is the impact on your health when you are able to pay attention to and follow these signals?

- Imagine yourself as a healthy 60 year old, 70 year old, 80 year old, and 90 year old. What steps can you take now to support your health for decades into the future?

- What can you do to support your family's health as well?

## *What I can do to be healthy – and what good health will enable me to do*

## MONEY

As you think about the money choices you will make in retirement, consider the following:

- To create a meaningful and happy retirement, would you need the same lifestyle you live now? One that's more expensive (in which case, how much more)? Or would a less expensive lifestyle be sufficient (in which case, how much less can you spend without seriously reducing your quality of life)?

- Do you enjoy making money just to make money? If so, would you like to include making money – whether as an investor, a business owner, or a part-time employee – part of your retirement?

- Do you enjoy thinking about money, or do you find finance-related deliberations boring or wearisome? Would you prefer to not have to think about money in your retirement? If so, how can you set up your retirement savings so that they require as little management as possible?

There are many good resources available about how to finance the kind of retirement you want. Some of the best of these appear in the Appendix at the back of this book.

Now shift your focus from what money can buy to how money can support you in becoming who you want to be and what you want to do for the world. Make notes on the following page, or in your journal, as you engage in this creative process.

From the foundation of security you create in your physical world, begin to envision a retirement life in which you make your dreams your reality. You might think about charities to support. You might think about starting your own service organization, foundation, support group, scholarship, or business.

Now imagine picking up a newspaper where the lead story is about something you have done to help or change the world.

- What is that story about? What did you do?

- What resources did you rally? Who helped you, and how?

- What challenges did you overcome to accomplish your goal?

- Did you have a vision of being able to help a person or a group? To right a wrong? To save a business or an institution?

- What has changed as a result of your action?

- What makes you most proud about how you made a difference?

- Did your action fulfill someone's dream, or create opportunities for others to dream?

Look at financial security as a way of freeing you to do, and be, a retiree who makes dreams come true.

## *How money can support what I can do for the world*

---

## SOCIETY

As young Boomers, we called for our political leaders to hear and reflect our cause, our vision, and our dreams. We remember when the issues mattered more to us than the politics. As an enlightened retiring Boomer, with your savvy, knowledge, and wisdom, is that still your goal? If you still dream of a world that reflects the best of who we are, can you turn your energy to that goal in your retirement?

Changing the world sounds impossible – too big, too hard, too entangled in politics. But if we think about changing one part of our world, that doesn't seem so unmanageable.

We can all recall moments of tragedy when people came together as one to rescue, to connect, and to reassure. Is there a way we enlightened retirees can model that caring energy in daily life? Can you imagine what part you could play in such a world?

We're all familiar with the phrase "think globally, act locally." We can apply that to our own lives. We care about the world, and we'll do what we can to save the part that is in front of us.

Think about the stories that appear every so often in the news: a whale has beached itself, or become lost in inland waters. One stranded whale will not be the making or breaking of the world, yet helpers flock to the scene and we watch avidly for news of rescue.

When the 35W bridge collapsed in Minneapolis in 2007, security and personal cameras recorded many survivors stumbling from their vehicles, looking around in shock, and then rushing *toward* the collapse. Setting aside their own bruises and fears, dozens turned toward their fellow victims, wanting to offer comfort, aid, or a hand to hold. Lives were saved by these actions and hearts were soothed by the selfless acts of those whose presence said to strangers, "We're in this together."

It is that spirit of caring, of rushing to the rescue, of trying our best to do what we can, that *does* make the difference in the world.

Our generation is beginning to retire while we're still at the peak of our wisdom and power. What is the sound of our social voice now?

You know yourself to be talented, skilled, and enormously capable. What causes do you care about? What would your impassioned voice sound like now, in your enlightened retirement, if you turned it to those causes? What might our joined voices sound like if we once more took up our dream of who we can be in the world?

On the following page, or in your journal, write your thoughts about ways you can act locally, use your voice, and be an example to engage our dream of how great the world can be.

In the U.S. alone, there are more than 78 million of us out here. If each one of us took one or two actions to save, redeem, and improve our local world, think of the power we would unleash into the universe.

In our retirement, as enlightened elders, what social legacy do we want to leave for our children? What do we want them to remember us speaking for, and speaking up about, long after we're gone?

As retirees, we have the ability, the time, and the voice to transform our society. We remember how we came together once with a voice for change. Can we do it again?

## *The social legacy I want to leave*

# III.

# Your Inner World

---

## WE ARE TRANSFORMERS

Transforming the world isn't always about moving the mountain off its base. We may not have drastically transformed society in the ways we thought we could. But because we were willing to listen to our inner voice, to remember and trust our feelings, and to dream locally as well as globally, we have effected some amazing changes. Today, more than at any other time in history, we have no tolerance for the exploitation and abuse of children. We understand and work toward gender equality in the workplace, and equal pay for equal work is now the law. Our mixed race President would not have been permitted to vote in parts of the United States back when we were born.

We remember pushing against indifference, intolerance, and injustice. We pushed – singly, in small groups, and in massive protests. We believed in ourselves, our dreams, and our right to ask for or demand change. We threw ourselves at life and dreamed big – not only for ourselves, but for our world. We all carried away a piece of that dream and have kept it quietly alive, banked like a small, glowing ember.

Retirement can be a time when we are called to bring these pieces back together, to breathe life back into the little spark we carry, to call up the dream and teach it to those coming after us.

Let yourself remember and reconnect with the parts of yourself that you cared about then, and still do.

- Recall a time when you wanted to change something you thought wasn't right, or fair, or good. Did you protest the VietNam war, rally for women's rights, organize for affirmative action, campaign for the ethical treatment of animals? What called to you?

- What issues or causes did you care about then that still aren't resolved today? Do they still have heat for you now? If so, what can you do now to move them forward?

- Do you feel that you walked away from something that is unfinished? Do you want to pick it up again now, with all your elder wisdom and power?

- Is there a new issue burning inside you that you want to help address?

- Do you know what causes your kids care about? Can you help them engage their own dream of making something better in the world?

Imagine a barren landscape before a garden is planted. Through one seed at a time, planted and tended, the landscape is transformed. In what ways can you, as a retiree, transform your world by one act, one person, one dream at a time? Record your thoughts on the following page or in your journal.

## *Ways I can become the seed of transformation one act, one person, or one dream at a time*

---

## GATHERING LESSONS

Each major event in our lives offers us an opportunity to learn and grow. Even the most difficult moments contain the seeds of growth and transformation. If we can become calm observers of the events in our lives, we can begin to see the lessons in them and let them prepare us for our future.

Thinking back over major events in your life will help you see how you have used them to learn and make positive changes. You may also find some unresolved issues that still contain lessons waiting to be gathered. As you think about the ideas in this section, you may want to make notes on the following page, or in your journal.

Gathering lessons is the first step; the second is to use those lessons well. For example:

- What essential lessons have you learned about life?

- In what ways are you wiser now than you ever expected?

- What life lessons do you want your children to learn?

- How can you help them develop a willingness to learn their own lessons?

- What lessons have best helped you prepare you for retirement?

- What have you learned about what your heart needs, who to be with, and where you feel safe and at home?

- What have you learned about what makes you happy?

- If you could go back to your 20-year-old self and see the hope and optimism in your eyes, what would you say to that person to keep their hope alive? To keep them safe? To keep them moving forward?

- What was your part of our great dream to change the world?

- What did you do – on your own or with other people – to make the world better? What did you want to do but never had a chance, until now?

- How would you best describe what you know that you can teach to others?

- How in your retirement years can you best share your wisdom? With whom? For what dream?

If accumulating and passing on lessons sounds too much like school, consider it a process of discovering your personal power. If you prefer, think of yourself as having gathered many bits of wisdom, for that is what well-learned lessons become.

## *How I'm wiser now, key lessons I've learned, and how I can share that wisdom*

## DREAM MAKERS

We Boomers knew instinctively that we were not here to just repeat familiar patterns. The power of our dreams gave us energy, ideas, visions of what could be.

Find a photo of one of your grandparents, put it next to a photo of you from the 60s or 70s, and show them to your children or grandchildren. These two pictures reveal vastly different life energies. The ancestral photo likely shows a somber, hard-working builder of a farm, city, road, bank, school, church, or family. Their serviceable, neutral toned clothes perfectly suit that life – the life of a worker. By comparison, the photo of you looks like science-fiction, and rightfully so. The person in this photo sees the stars. This is the photo of a dreamer.

Had we asked our grandparents what they dreamed of, the response might have been: "I don't have time for dreams; there's work to do." Ask our parents about their dreams, and they might say, "Our dream was to give you a comfortable childhood and help you become a successful adult."

Yet the greatest inventions, works of art, and scientific discoveries originate from people who listen to their dreams. To suppress our dreams is to deny a part of ourselves.

Assume for the moment that your childhood dreams are a message to you about what gives your life joy and meaning.

- Recall what you wanted to be when you grew up. What did you tell others about that occupation? How did you imagine you would look and feel as that person? What images were in your head about the person you would become? To what degree have you become that person now?

- What books did you read and what movies did you enjoy when you were young? Did you identify with – or want to be – a particular character? To what degree have you become that character?

- What dreams did you have for yourself in your 20s and 30s? Did you want a college education, a particular career, marriage, parenthood? Which of those dreams became reality? What did you do to help make them real?

- Can you remember one particular vision or dream that became so important to you, so compelling, so large, that it felt almost inevitable? Can you recall the intensity of feeling, of energy, that infused this vision?

- Do you have a similarly important and compelling vision for yourself now? For your children? For the world?

Now, using your visioning skills, envision your own ideal retirement. Let yourself be detailed, specific, enthusiastic, and intense. Then, on the following page or in your journal, write down, or draw, your vision in all its grandeur, glory, and specificity.

In retirement, you will be called to stand at the gate where dreams and visions live, to hold it open, and to show the way to what can be. Now is the perfect time to become a dream maker.

## *My ideal retirement*

# RELATIONSHIPS.

As a retiree, your circle of friends may change. You may relocate or travel extensively. In retirement you can choose how to live, whom to live with, what to do, and with whom to do it. Your choices about relationships now may more deeply reflect your wishes, your passion, and your sense of purpose, rather than who lives nearby or whom you work with.

Just as relationships change in retirement, you may also find yourself spending periods of quiet time alone. In such states of quiet and contemplation, it is possible to find acceptance, grace, serenity, and peace. How might peaceful time alone, as you develop and deepen your relationship with yourself, add a new dimension to your retirement years? Make notes in your journal, or on the following page, about this and the following considerations.

Reflect on your closest and most important relationships for a few minutes, then ask yourself which person or people in your life you most want to be with:

- In a crisis

- On a desert island

- In celebrating a joyous occasion or event

- in simply relaxing and doing nothing

- in the final months and years of your life

Now think about each of the people you currently spend time with. Write down their names, and, for each name, ask yourself:

- Is this someone you look forward to seeing?

- Is this person important to you?

- Are you important to them?

- Does this person enrich or energize your life?

- Do you maintain a relationship with this person out of a sense of duty, obligation, or politeness?

- Can this person help you align with your retirement dreams? How?

Lastly, on the following page, or in your journal, record the qualities you most value in relationships, both those you have now and those you desire in the future. Then write down the qualities you most value in the people with whom you currently have positive, energizing relationships. Underneath these, make a list of the most valuable qualities you can offer others in relationships with them.

All relationships – with others and with yourself – connect you with your heart, your dreams, your purpose, and your passion. In your retirement years, you have the freedom, the wisdom, and the choice to relate with others in alignment with all you dream for yourself and for our world.

*Relationships – what I value, want more of, and can give*

## UNIVERSAL CONNECTIONS

Connections nurture, sustain, and enrich us. They are both a spiritual inheritance and a legacy.

Now we have mostly finished raising our families, growing our careers, and managing what might be called the business of life. As we've matured, we have begun to return to our inner life once more. It is here, in our hearts and spirits, that we will again find our connection to our deeper self, to each other, and to our dreams.

Imagine that for one day you will leave a visible trail behind you, like a glowing rope. Imagine that rope unfurling behind you, winding its way around your community and encircling everyone you come in contact with. Can you see how profoundly you are connected to the world, even as you go about your daily life?

Now imagine that you go to one of your favorite places in your city or town and sit still for an entire day. Everyone who comes in contact with you has their own visible glowing rope, which will encircle you when you converse, or touch, or even just when your eyes meet. At the end of the day, how many strands of rope are touching you?

Now imagine how many of these glowing ropes of connection touch you in a single week.

You are at the center of a web of connections. Look outward at all the glowing strands of rope that reach from your heart out into the world — toward other people, places, and energies. Do you see how each person to whom you are connected is also at the center of their own web? Can you envision just how vast our connection is to all living things?

When you think about people who have been there for you in your life, or who have appeared when you most needed them, what do you feel? Are they aware of the extent of their impact on your life? If not, how can you let them know now? It is never too late to connect. Use your journal, or the following page, to note how these small and large connections have made a difference in your life. This may take the form of a list, a description, or even a drawing with you at the center and all of your connections radiating outward.

What might be the impact on the world if the 78 million of us Boomers all used our ropes of connection to pull hearts closer together?

## *Connections that made a difference*

## WHAT DOES THE WORLD NEED FROM YOU?

Often what the world needs from us is not some big, grandiose, highly visible action. More often it is the small, daily, loving acts that make the biggest difference. The world needs us to model loving family relationships and friendships, and the wise and compassionate treatment of everyone we encounter. From this foundation, we will find the energy and resources to change the world.

As you look inside yourself and ponder 20 or more post-retirement years of healthy, active living, a large question emerges: *What does the world need from me?*

In retirement you will have the power to re-invent yourself in ways the world desperately needs.

Suspend for a moment any thoughts you have, or teachings you have learned, about the meaning of life. Imagine that you purposely, deliberately chose this life you have right now. Then ask yourself: *Why did I come here, now, into this life? Did I come to be with someone in particular, to do something special, to fulfill a promise, to leave a legacy?*

Think of your close family members and your closest friends and colleagues. Imagine that they, too, deliberately chose this life, and this time, to be with you. What about you was so important to them, that they came to be part of your life?

Now ask yourself these questions, and write your thoughts in your journal or on the following page.

- What do you want to pass on to others, or to the world at large, before you leave this life?

- How do you want history – or your friends, family, and descendents – to remember you?

- Is there an unmet personal goal that you thought you would accomplish before you die? Are there parts of that goal that you can still achieve? Is there a way to restructure your goal so that you can make it a part of your retirement plan? Are there people whom you can rally to help you achieve it? As long as you're still here, it's not too late.

- Are there relationships you want to heal, or new ones you want to form?

- What do you not want to leave undone before you go?

During our work years, it is usually clear what our employers, friends, and family need from us. Now, as a retiree with time, resources, and choice at hand, you can answer that deeper call of what the world needs from you. We Boomers know that somewhere within us lies our personal piece of the answer to that call. What is it that you came to do for the world?

## *What I came to do for the world*

---

# IV.

# Synthesizing and Manifesting

---

Your wisdom extends far beyond the physical realm, and involves the spiritual energy that can enrich your retirement and bring your dreams closer. Three powerful ways of engaging this energy are creativity, meditation, and manifesting peace.

## CREATING

All of us have the innate ability to be creative. As children we effortlessly created imaginary friends, fantasy worlds, improbable scenarios. We built kingdoms with Legos, drew alternate universes with crayons, made tree forts and doll houses. Creating came naturally to us.

Now, as retirement approaches, reconnecting with your creativity gives you the power to once again experience and transmit joy, while adding something new to the world.

Creating is often about looking at something familiar in a new way. When you are thinking, or daydreaming, do you come up with new ways of doing things? An invention that you'd like to see developed? A story you'd like to write? A scene you'd like to photograph? Do you have ideas for ways something could work better? Do you make up songs in your head? Cook without a recipe?

Think about all the times you've helped your children learn something difficult, like skating, riding a bike, or multiplying triple-digit numbers. Can you see the influence of your creativity in explaining things several different ways, in coming up with examples, and in asking helpful questions?

Think about times when you were completely stuck as you were trying to do something the "normal" way, and you came up with your own, better way of accomplishing the task. Creativity isn't only about making something. It is very much about the mindset you bring to your everyday life and, by extension, to the world.

Observe yourself for the next week as you go about your daily activities. Be aware of ways in which you create for those around you – at work, in your family, with your friends. You can make a note on the following page, or in your journal, each time you create a different way of doing something, think of a new solution to a problem, or help someone gain insight or knowledge. Then think about the ways in which retirement can provide you with the opportunity to look at the familiar with new eyes.

In retirement you will have the time, energy and resources to create something you love, to bring something new or better into the world. Create, and feel yourself connected to the flow of life.

## *Ways I am creative*

## MEDITATING

Remember when you were a kid and could get lost for minutes – or hours – in a fantasy or game? Remember how time seemed to stop, and how the "normal" world seemed to recede into the background? In those moments you were in a meditative state, where your heart, mind, and body were all in sync, all absorbed in the activity of the moment and connected to the realm of your dreams. Another meditative state is in that drifting time between sleep and wakefulness, where you're vaguely conscious but floating with your dreams.

Let retirement be a time to re-experience these states of focus and enjoyment. If you do not already have a regular practice of relaxation and meditation, why not establish one as you retire?

The benefits of meditation are well documented. It brings the brainwave pattern into an alpha state, a level of consciousness that promotes healing. It improves concentration, increases oxygen flow, slows your breathing, helps lower blood pressure, reduces anxiety, decreases muscle tension, enhances the immune system, and leads to deep levels of relaxation. A consistent practice of simple meditation can do much to support your psychological and physiological well-being.

Try doing this simple form of meditation for 15 – 45 minutes a day. While seated comfortably, close your eyes, relax your body, and slow your breathing to a comfortable, even rate. As your mind wanders, just bring it back to your breathing. It may be helpful to repeat a sound, focus on soft music, or count to yourself to help return your focus to your breath. This will get easier with practice.

If you like, imagine a beautiful natural setting that makes you feel peaceful and happy. Envision yourself there, seeing it through a child's eyes, letting the peace and serenity envelop you. In this state, you are open to relaxation, intuition, and active dreaming.

If you can meditate for even ten or fifteen minutes a day, what to you think might change?

- Might you have more energy?

- Would you more clearly remember your dreams?

- Could you generate more creative ideas?

- What might happen if you chose to meditate with someone else, or in a group?

Try meditating once a day for at least two weeks, then use the following page, or your personal journal, to make notes or drawings about what you experienced during your meditation.

Our childhood ability to achieve meditative states has not been lost. We can now embrace it as retirees. Consider how a simple daily practice of complete relaxation and opening to the voice of your dreams could energize your retirement.

## *Experiences in meditation*

## MANIFESTING PEACE

Retirement offers us a peace we may not have experienced since childhood, if ever. As the pressures of work and family ease in our retirement years, we can return our thoughts to what a peaceful world might be like, and open our hearts to helping create it.

Peace comes from within. It is a form of power we can send out into the world, share, and embody. It is a choice we can make, over and over. It is a way of thinking and behaving that we can pass along to our children. It is a force within us to be manifested.

Each of us has the ability to become Gandhi-like in our own life, and to model that way of being for those coming behind us. We can each become a peacemaker in the way we send energy into the world, the words we use, and the way we treat people around us. In myriad large and small ways, you can become a force for peace.

What impact could Boomers have on the world if each of us becomes a peacemaker, becomes the energy and intention of peace?

Consider the story of the two wolves. The wise elder explains to his grandson, "Inside me there live two wolves who are always fighting. One wolf is evil; he is guilt, anger, envy, regret, greed, arrogance, self-pity, resentment, inferiority, lies, false pride, superiority, self-doubt, and ego. The second wolf is good; he is joy, peace, love, hope, serenity, humility, kindness, benevolence, empathy, generosity, truth, compassion and faith. It is a terrible fight and the same fight is going on inside every other person, too." The grandson is thoughtful for several minutes, then asks his grandfather which of the two wolves will win the fight. The elder smiles kindly and replies, "whichever one I feed."

What does peace look like? Physically we know it to be the absence of violence and war. But spiritually and emotionally, what is it? How would you describe peace to an alien being who had no concept of it? Use the following page, or your journal, to write or draw your vision of peace. You may come up with a new phrase, symbol, or picture. Let your imagination go.

As young Boomers we made a lot of noise about "peace now." Is that something we still want to do now, as retirees? What would that sound like? Is there a picture of peace, a voice of peace, that we can leave our children and our grandchildren?

When we become peace, manifest it in our lives, and model it for our children, the world will move inexorably toward it.

*What peace looks like to me*

---

# V.

# Your Unique Legacy

---

The founders of the United States came together in the 1700s to create a new nation built on their dream of what that world could be. They imagined something that had never been, shared their visions for what the result might be, and dreamed beyond anything that had so far existed. They combined their skills, experiences, and dreams into a living legacy their descendents still embrace today.

The same opportunity exists for Boomers right now. Separately and collectively, we have carried the vision of a better, more just, more peaceful world. In our maturity we now possess the knowledge and the strength to build that new world.

## QUESTION EVERYTHING – AGAIN

If there was one characteristic that defined us as younger Baby Boomers, it was our willingness to question everything. Over and over, we asked ourselves and others, *Why? Why not?* and *What if?* Questioning everything was part of our early call for a world of peace, equality, justice, and freedom. It can also be our mantra in our retirement.

We still hold our vision of a better world. Now our commitment to question everything, combined with our maturity and wisdom, can do much to make that vision our reality.

- Can you remember when you first began to hear your inner voice asking questions – wanting reasons and explanations for how things were? Was it in school, in your family, or with your friends?

- Can you think of instances when you felt instinctively that the status quo might be outdated or insufficient for you?

- Can you recall questioning external things, such as other peoples' rules, expectations, and authority? How did it change your life? Others' lives? The rules themselves?

- Can you reflect on times when others questioned you? How did you react? Did it change your feelings about them, or your relationship to them?

Boomers are known for questioning rules, norms, standards, expectations, and ways of doing things. As you've matured, has the the nature of your questioning changed? When you are working through an issue, or exploring new ground, where do you go for the incisive questions that will help you? Do you consult your spouse, a friend, clergy, self-help material, or a therapist? Do you pray, meditate, take a personal retreat, write, paint, build, exercise? The resources and people that have helped you discover and ask your questions will be invaluable to you in retirement.

Because retirement offers you the opportunities and freedom to change many aspects of your life, you can now question everything again. Don't just question others and the world, however. Also spend some time questioning again your desires, preferences, passions, and dreams. This will help you clarify them, better understand them, take them more seriously, amend them, and, in some cases, replace them with something even better.

In retirement, maintain your curious mind, and give yourself permission to again ask, *"Why?" "Why not?"* and *"What if?"* The following page, or a page in your journal, awaits your questions.

*Why? Why not? What if?*

## FEARLESS THINKING

Fear in the animal world is a necessary protective mechanism. It can keep an animal safe in a wildly unpredictable world. In early human history it served the same function for us. But in current times, our physical world is safer than at any time in our history. It is in our emotional world where fear is more likely to move in and take up residence.

A life change as large as retirement can be frightening. We may have fears about money, health, or our life's purpose.

But retirement is surely not the first time you have faced and conquered fear. You can look to those times in your past when you have been fearful about something – passing a test, starting a new job, relocating, getting married, having children, or facing financial ups and downs.

- How did you face those fears?

- Did you talk them through with someone?

- Did you consult professionals or self-help resources?

- Did you hold fast to a vision or a goal?

- Did you rely on a spiritual practice? How successful were you in navigating and conquering your fears?

It is useful to think about fear as a natural pause built into our thoughts and actions. Whenever we embark on something new – a commitment, a change, an adventure – there is an element of the unknown involved, and a momentary pause can be healthy. It gives us a chance to review, to reflect, and to make sure we are as prepared as we can be. In this way, fear is a helpful companion, so long as we keep it from overwhelming our dreams.

Imagine people who stand on the bridge before bungee jumping, or on the deck before plunging into the ocean to scuba dive. Or remember yourself leaping off the high dive for the first time, riding your bike down that forbidden hill, or going out on that first date. These are ways that life pulls you forward, and in each there is an element of fear, giving you pause and sending up caution flags.

Reflect on such incidents in your life.

- Did fear try to keep you from going ahead?

- What made you decide to go ahead anyway?

- What technique did you use to allay your fear, such as talking with someone, prayer or meditation, determination, or a specific goal?

- At the moment you decided to go ahead, what happened to your fear?

- How much fear remained the second, or the third, time you took the same action?

Remembering how you have dealt with the caution flags of fear in your past, and then gone ahead with your life, can be a valuable resource as you embrace retirement.

You have been on the journey to your retirement for a long time and it will take you to a new world, full of adventures and your dreams. Fears may arise along the way, but you have experience and success in going right ahead toward the adventure.

Use the following page or your journal to describe your fears about retirement, how you have handled and conquered fear in the past, and how you can face your retirement with a spirit of adventure that supercedes fear.

The less fear you carry, the more light you can hold and shine outward into the world.

## *How I faced and handled my fears*

---

## TELL YOUR STORY

Each of us has a life story that, in some unique way, is a thread in the great human tapestry. We all come from a heritage of story-tellers, and will leave a legacy in the chronicles of our family, our friends, and our community.

What are the key events in your own life, and what story or stories do they tell? On the next page, or in your journal, lay out the most important events in your life. Here are some ways you might do this:

- Think of these events as chapters of a book (complete with titles, if you like), or episodes of a TV series.

- Tell your story by topic or aspect of your life: early childhood, school, college, work, family, etc.

- Tell it by location: your hometown, cities you've lived in, places you've traveled, and places you hope to explore.

- Tell it by focusing on each of the key people in your life: your parents, your siblings, your children, your partner, your best friends.

Once you have the arc of your life story laid out, look at if from beginning to end. Think of it as an epic journey. Is there a pattern to the big events in your life? What lesson or lessons does the story teach?

Think about the major turning points in your life.

- Is there a pattern to when those points occurred, how you reacted to them, the people you were with, or what you did?

- Can you identify major lessons that occurred during these turning points? Major decisions you had to make? Recurring issues or challenges?

- What coping skills did you employ? Did they change over time? Did you gain confidence or wisdom from your experiences?

- At major crossroads on your path, did you experience particular wake-up calls, epiphanies, or insights?

- As you look back over this unfolding story of your life, can you identify the themes and the underlying flow?

Imagine that your story is a life manual for your descendents. What do you want them to learn, to appreciate, to avoid, to celebrate?

What would be the best title for this story of your life?

How do you want your story to end? What do you want it to say to those who come after you?

Our Boomer saga has millions of chapters. Yours is waiting to be told.

## *My life and what it means and teaches*

---

# VI.

# Do what you can from where you are

---

Part of our Boomer path has been about learning to stand *in light*. Our journey to a fulfilling and meaningful retirement includes activating the light in us, and then shining it outward.

As we enter retirement, we can consciously shine our light on our descendents and into the world as enlightened seniors.

## ACTS OF KINDNESS

Kindness is the power we all possess to engage the energy of connection without words. Kindness focuses the heart's energy and is self-fulfilling: the more you give, the more you have to give, and the more you are likely to receive. Kindness returns to the sender, multiplied and inexhaustible.

As you consider the following questions, make notes on the following page, or in your journal.

- When you extend kindness to someone, what do you observe about their reaction? Are they surprised, pleased, embarrassed, grateful?

- Can you think of situations in which your kindness may have changed someone's life? Someone's relationship with you?

- What childhood memories do you have of someone being kind to you?

- What people or circumstances regularly elicit your kindness now?

- As a retiree, with more time and freedom at hand, do you think the way you practice kindness will change? What might those changes be? How might they affect those around you?

- Can you think of an instance when someone's kindness changed your life? What was the event? How did it make you feel? Who was the person – a friend, a teacher, a parent, an elder?

- How might you make acts of kindness a part of your daily life in retirement? What would be the impact of those acts?

- What part can kindness play in your dreams and goals for a better world?

*Acts of kindness …. then, now, and into the future*

## GRATITUDE

Gratitude is one of the most elegant and powerful human acts. Available equally to all, it costs nothing; it can change lives and, thus, the world. Expressing gratitude empowers us, connects us, and encourages the flow of positive energy all around us.

As Boomers, most of us have had many advantages in our lives. And we will enjoy a quality and length of retirement unprecedented in our society. It's fair to say, then, that we face an equally unprecedented opportunity to engage the power of gratitude.

As a retiree, with a long life behind you and a promising future ahead of you, make a list of gifts and blessings. Feel free to include your family, your friends, your home, your health, your successes, your skills and knowledge, your intuition, your ability to create, your ability to dream, and anything else that occurs to you. Use the following page, or your journal, for this list.

Now, review this list briefly. The longer the list, the more opportunities you have to express your gratitude directly.

- Whom do you especially appreciate in your life?

- How do you let them know?

- Do you make it a practice to thank your partner, your children, and your friends for their presence and love in your life? How might they feel if you did this routinely? How might *you* feel?

- Would the energy of gratitude increase the joy in your and their lives?

Of course, expressing gratitude doesn't require a particular recipient. We can also make a practice of sending our gratitude out into the world at large. This keeps the flow of energy circulating, and increases the opportunity for giving and receiving continued blessings.

How can you embody the spirit of gratitude from this day forward to become a shining point of light in the world?

Do what you can from where you are

## *I am grateful for ….*

---

# Seeker, Pathfinder, Guardian

We began in our youth with raw energy and enthusiasm, with a collective voice for change, and with a dream of making things better. As we enter retirement and look around for each other again, let us think about the world we leave for our descendents. Let us now, in our maturity, re-define our dream and leave it for our children's children. Let us be known as the generation that cared about peace and still does, as the generation that believed in equality and still does, as the generation that worked for social justice and still does.

Help our descendents to know us as a generation that cared about the world they will inherit from us. Let them see us as the generation that took a different path, that believed that each and every voice matters. Let our descendents look at our lives and say, "Yes, my ancestor was one of those crazy Baby Boomers. Thank goodness."

Every great adventure story has several important elements: a seeker who looks beyond what is to what might be, a pathfinder who explores and searches for the way, and a guardian who watches over the travelers and holds open the gates to tomorrow. We Boomers took on all of these roles. In retirement, we can practice them once again with skill, integrity, and gusto.

We Boomers explored new ways of thinking, of interacting, and now of retiring. We've not let "how it has always been" get in the way of looking for new answers to old questions, new questions to ask, and new paths to explore.

We know what a better world looks like; we've carried that dream with us our entire lives. Each of us has a piece of the dream. Now, as the elders of our tribe, we can come together and help our descendents see it. We can hold open the gates, having been the seekers and pathfinders.

A single generation may not be able to save the world. But one determined, visionary generation can make improving the world a dream worth keeping alive. If each of us fulfills *that* legacy, we will have brought forward millions of dreamers.

Hold the gate open for the dreamers who are coming behind you.

# Appendix
# Recommended "How To" Retirement Resources

---

*Live It Up Without Outliving Your Money!: Getting the Most From Your Investments in Retirement* by Paul Merriman.
Wiley, 2nd edition, June 2008.

*Retirement Income Redesigned: Master Plans for Distribution: An Adviser's Guide for Funding Boomers' Best Years* by Harold Evensky (editor) and Deena B. Katz (editor.
Bloomberg Press, April 2006

*Ready...Set...Retire!: Financial Strategies for the Rest of Your Life* by Raymond J. Lucia and Dale Fetherling.
Hay House, March 2008.

*Yes, You Can Still Retire Comfortably!: The Baby-Boom Retirement Crisis and How to Beat It* by Ben Stein and Phil DeMuth.
New Beginnings Press; 1st edition, August 2006.

*Your Retirement, Your Way: Why It Takes More Than Money to Live Your Dream* by Alan Bernstein and John Trauth.
McGraw-Hill; 1st edition. September 2006.

*The New Retirement: The Ultimate Guide to the Rest of Your Life* by Jan Cullinane and Cathy Fitzgerald
Rodale Books, July 7, 2004.

*Looking Forward: An Optimist's Guide to Retirement* by Ellen Freudenheim
Harry N. Abrams, November 2004.

*How Much Is Enough – Balancing Today's Needs with Tomorrow's Retirement Goals* by Diana McCurdy.
Wiley, September 2005.

*Get a Life: You Don't Need a Million to Retire Well* by Ralph E. Warner.
NOLO; 5th edition, November 2004.

*How to Retire Happy, Wild, and Free: Retirement Wisdom That You Won't Get from Your Financial Advisor* by Ernie J. Zelinski.
Ten Speed Press, March 2004.

*The Wall Street Journal. Complete Retirement Guidebook: How to Plan It, Live It and Enjoy It* by Glenn Ruffenach and Kelly Greene.
Three Rivers Press, June 2007.

*Transitions: Making Sense of Life's Changes, Revised 25th Anniversary Edition* bu William Bridges.
Da Capo Press; 2nd expanded updated edition, August 2004.

*Your Complete Retirement Planning Road Map: A Comprehensive Action Plan for Securing IRAs, 401(k)s, and Other Retirement Plans for Yourself and Your Family* by Ed Slott.
Ballantine Books, December 2007.

*What Color Is Your Parachute? for Retirement: Planning Now for the Life You Want* by Richard Nelson Bolles and John E. Nelson.
Ten Speed Press, May 2007.

*How to Love Your Retirement: Advice from Hundreds of Retirees (Hundreds of Heads Survival Guides)* by Hundreds of Heads (author), Barbara Waxman (editor) and Bob Mendelson (editor).
Hundreds of Heads Books, August 2006.

*Retirement: Wise And Witty Advice For Making It The Next Great Adventure* by Natasha Josefowitz.
Blue Mountain Press, February 2005.

*Women, Men, and Money: The Four Keys for Using Money to Nourish Your Relationship, Bankbook and Soul* by William Fran Jr. Devine.
Three Rivers Press, 1999.

*The Courage to be Rich: Creating a Life of Material and Spiritual Abundance* by Suze Orman.
Riverhead Trade, 1st edition, December 2001.

www.ingramcontent.com/pod-product-compliance
Lightning Source LLC
Chambersburg PA
CBHW051044030426
42339CB00006B/192